Improvising Lead Guitar

Beginner Plus

by

Tony Skinner

Registry RGT standard: GRADE ONE

A CIP record for this publication is available from the British Library.

ISBN: 1-898466-35-1

© 2000 Registry Publications

Published in Great Britain by

Registry House, Churchill Mews, Dennett Rd, Croydon, Surrey, CR0 3JH

Typesetting by

Take Note Publishing Ltd., Lingfield, Surrey

Printed in Great Britain by Columbian Press, Kenley, Surrey.

Contents

CD running order

Introduction

The purpose of this book is to help you develop skills in lead guitar improvisation.

Improving your skills in this area will help you develop your ability in creating your own solos in a wide range of musical styles. For any guitarist wishing to join a band this is an essential skill. However, this ability is often difficult to acquire unless you have someone to play the backing chords for you to improvise over. Fortunately, the accompanying CD provides a full band backing track for all the chord sequences shown within this book.

By playing along with the CD you'll be able to hear exactly how your lead guitar improvisation sounds in a real band setting.

All the scales you need to start your improvising are shown later in the book, and are demonstrated at practice and performance speeds on the CD.

get tuned

Before you start playing you'll need to get your guitar in tune.

The CD tuning guide (Track I) gives you the pitch of each string starting with the low E string. Turn the machine head until the note from this string matches the pitch produced on the recording. Follow this procedure for the remaining strings.

Although this may be easier said than done, do persevere as it will help develop your sense of pitch.

If you find it really difficult to tune your guitar, then ask a musical friend or teacher to help you. Alternatively, investing in an electronic tuner could prove to be a great frustration beater – although you should beware of becoming *too* reliant on such a device.

get graded

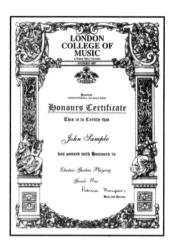

This book is structured in line with the Registry Of Guitar Tutors' electric guitar examination syllabus. It covers all you need to know about the *lead guitar* section of the examination at Grade One level. The book provides an ideal study aid for those preparing to take the RGT *Grade One* electric guitar examination; however the book is designed so that it can be used by all budding guitar players whether intending to take the examination or not.

If you wish to obtain a FREE electric guitar examination syllabus, send a stamped addressed envelope to: Registry of Guitar Tutors, Registry House, Churchill Mews, Croydon, Surrey, CR0 3JH, United Kingdom.

How to improvise

Improvisation. It's a term that's often bandied about by musicians – but what does it really mean? It's not simply about playing scales up and down, neither is it about creating melodies off the top of your head without reference to scales. The truth lies somewhere between the two, and the ideal mix needs the addition of a few other ingredients as well – such as the use of repetition, phrasing and stylistic interpretation. So whilst guitar improvising might typically be defined as *making up a lead solo on the spot*, in reality there is a readily identifiable structure and form behind this concept.

know your scales

To solo over any chord sequence you'll need to know the relevant scale. This will define the choice of notes that will fit with the backing chords. Before you start any improvisation you should play through the appropriate scale several times until you are *totally* familiar with it. Remember, it's the scale that sets the range of notes you can play. You should know it so well that you can relax whilst playing it, and be free to focus your attention on *using* the scale to make an interesting solo. So it's a good idea to begin by learning your scales thoroughly – that means forwards, backwards and inside out! Five of the most useful scales for early stage players are displayed later on in this book.

riff and rest

> "Create short melodic phrases... don't be scared to leave gaps"

Once you're sure that you know your way around the scales you can start to improvise some lead work over one of the backing chord sequences that are shown in this book (and featured on the CD).

Try to invent short phrases rather than a continuous flurry of notes and don't be scared to leave gaps. You don't need to play all the notes of the scale, nor in any particular order (and certainly not in the set scale order). Once you have learnt the scale, the aim is to use it in a melodically inventive and creative way and try to avoid sounding too scale-like in your playing.

trust your ear

> "There's no need to worry about hitting a wrong note...just rely on your scale."

All the notes of the correct scale will fit over all of the backing chords – although admittedly some will sound better than others. Let your ears guide you as to which ones sound best. Rest assured that none of the notes within the scale will totally clash with the backing chords. Play some notes that are NOT in the scale against the backing track and you'll soon hear the difference – the ones outside the scale will sound completely wrong. As long as you've chosen the correct scale, there's no need to worry about playing a wrong note; all of the notes in the scale WILL fit over the chords – although some will sound more harmonically *resolved* than others over particular chords. If you hit a note that sounds too unresolved for your liking simply move smoothly and deliberately onto the next note (above or below) in the scale and this will always sound fine.

Plectrum technique   *how to pick*

How do you hold this handy little device? Well, it's not just a case of grabbing hold of it and hoping for the best. If you hold the plectrum the wrong way it can slow down your playing for years to come. The best method is to grip the plectrum between the thumb and index finger. Position the plectrum so that its point is about half a centimetre beyond the fingertip. If you let too much poke through it may snag on the string; too little and you may miss the string totally. Also, be careful how you grip the plectrum. If you use too much pressure your hand muscles will tighten and so reduce your fluency, but don't hold it so loosely that you keep dropping it.

In order that your wrist can move freely, hold the plectrum so that it is in-line with your fingernail. Avoid holding it at right angles to your index finger as this will cause your wrist to lock. To gain speed and fluency, it's essential that the picking movement stems from the wrist NOT from the elbow. Unless you're trying to produce a particular effect, you should always alternate down and up plectrum strokes. To only pick in one direction is akin to trying to run by hopping on one leg. If you've never used *alternate picking* before, it may feel more difficult at first, but in the long run this technique will allow you to achieve much greater speed and fluency.

Stages to improvising

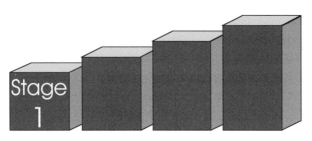

get in key

"Select a scale that fits with the key of the song."

Before you begin to play any lead you'll need to identify the *key* of the song. Since nearly all songs begin with the tonic (i.e. home key) chord, the easiest method is to check the first chord of the song. For example:

- if the first chord is E minor, you can be pretty certain that the song is in the key of E minor, and so your lead playing should come from the E natural minor scale;

- the A pentatonic minor scale is simply a shortened minor scale and so it fits well with a sequence in the key of A minor – e.g. one that starts with an A minor chord;

- if the first chord is A major then you should use the A major scale;

- the G pentatonic major scale is simply a shortened major scale and so it fits well with a sequence in the key of G major – e.g. one that starts with a G major chord;

- the blues scale is designed to be used over bluesy chord sequences, which normally start with a dominant 7th chord. So if a song begins with an E7 chord, then the E blues scale would be a good scale to use.

It's important to remember all this, as playing the wrong scale over a chord sequence will sound pretty dire. It doesn't matter how fast and flashy your lead playing is; if you're using the wrong scale then you're certain to hit notes that will clash with the backing chords. Be particularly careful not to get confused between the two different 'A' scales: only use the A pentatonic minor scale over songs that start with the chord of A minor; never use it with any songs that begin with an A major chord.

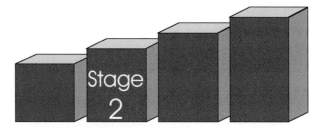

try the scale

"Practise the scale and experiment with rhythms."

Once you're sure which scale to use, start by simply playing the scale up and down over the backing track so that you can begin to hear the overall sound (or tonality) of the key. Then, rather than playing the scale in *straight* time, experiment by playing some notes quickly whilst allowing others to ring on. You'll notice that this sounds far more musical and inventive than the *straight* scale, even though you're still playing the same notes in the same order. So to recap: begin by playing a straight scale and then vary the rhythm – lengthening some notes and shortening others. But do remember that the scale only determines the range of notes that fit the chords in the key. Once you're familiar with the sound of the scale you should try to use it in a melodically inventive and creative way. Try to avoid just playing straight up and down the scale and sounding too scale-like in your playing.

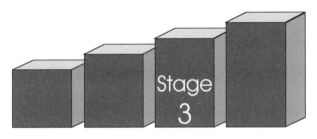

do it again

"Use repetition to give your solo structure"

By repeating clusters of notes you can start to develop melodic phrasing and structure. Once you have a phrase that you like, try and vary it slightly when you repeat it – that way it will sound fresh, whilst still giving the listener something recognisable to latch onto.

Try to leave gaps between your phrases – so that the music has space to breathe. Remember that it's not always necessary to play turbo-speed licks to make a great guitar solo – the choice of just a few carefully selected and well-executed notes can often have far greater emotional impact. Sometimes the saying 'less is more' gives the best clue to establishing the right *feel* for a

piece of music. It all depends on the type of music. It's up to you to listen carefully to the accompaniment and use your own musical judgement to decide upon the best form of stylistic interpretation.

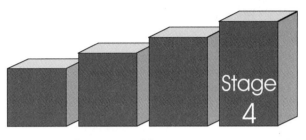

now phrase it

"Just playing scales isn't enough to make a great solo."

Experiment with the scales and try to improvise your own solos over the backing tracks. Although you can begin by simply playing the correct scale up and down over the backing track (so that you can begin to hear the overall sound and tonality of the key), always bear in mind that just playing scales up and down isn't enough to make a good solo. Scales simply determine the notes which can be utilised in any key. It's up to you to create melodically and rhythmically interesting phrases from the scale. The important thing is to let your ears and intuition, rather than your fingers, guide you. Before you begin to play, listen carefully to at least one sequence of the backing track in order to choose an appropriate style of solo, then try to make your improvisation fit in with the *rhythm* and *style* of the backing.

Reading scales

All the scales within this book are illustrated using the Registry Of Guitar Tutors' unique *Guitarograph* system. This incorporates tablature, standard musical notation, scale formula and fingerboard information all in one diagram. As the guitarograph illustrates the same information in this unique combination of four different systems there should be no doubt how to play any scale.

guitarograph

tablature

The tablature is shown on the left of the guitarograph, with horizontal lines representing the strings (with the high E string being string 1), and the numbers on the string lines referring to the frets.

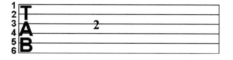

musical notation

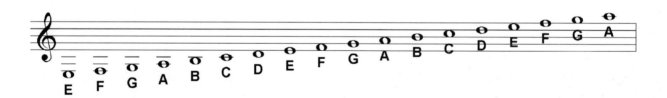

The middle section of each guitarograph illustrates the scale in standard musical notation.

fingerboard diagram

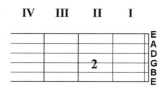

The fingerboard diagram is shown on the right of the guitarograph with horizontal lines representing the strings.

Vertical lines represent the frets; with fret numbers shown in Roman numerals.

The numbers on the horizontal lines show the recommended fingering.

scale formula

A	B	C#	D	E	F#	G#	A
1	2	3	4	5	6	7	8

Above each guitarograph is a scale formula which lists the pitch of the notes together with their interval numbers (in relaton to the major scale with the same starting pitch).

The scale formulae will help you identify the differences in construction between the various scales and help you learn the names of the notes that you are playing.

A thorough knowledge of the notes on the fingerboard provides a sound foundation for developing your guitar playing in the future. Spending a little time memorising the notes within each scale, and where they occur on the fingerboard, will prove to be a worthwhile investment of time.

Scale fingering

Fingerings have been chosen which are likely to be the most effective for the widest range of players at this level. There are, however, a variety of alternative fingerings and fingerboard positions that could be used for most scales and you should feel free to explore any other systematic fingerings that produce a good musical result.

using all four

In general you should use a 'one finger per fret' technique. This involves using all four fingers of the fretting hand when necessary. There is often a great temptation not to use the fourth finger as it may feel weaker than the others. However, this will mean that you will be operating at only 75% of your potential. Having said that, you may discover that several very famous and respected players of the past relied almost solely on the use of only three fingers. However this doesn't mean that this is going to be the right method for you – particularly if you ever want to venture into the more technically demanding styles of guitar playing.

> **"Why use only three fingers... when you've got four at your disposal"**

- By not incorporating the fourth finger into your technique it will take many more hours of practice to play the same complex riff compared to someone who is using all their fingers.

- If your fourth finger does feel weak this is often because it hasn't been used much before! In other words, if you don't use your fourth finger it will feel weak and therefore you won't feel like using it – a classic 'catch 22' situation.

- Once you do start using the little finger regularly it will develop strength and eventually you will feel as confident using it as you do your other fingers.

at the edge

With all scales, you should stretch your fingers out so that you can press with your fingertips at the very edge of the frets – right next to the fretwire. This way you will not only avoid fretbuzz, but also you won't have to press too hard.

> **"The closer to the fretwire you press... the less pressure you need to apply"**

- If you press in the middle of the fret (away from the fretwire) you will find that it's much harder to achieve clarity.

- When playing two or more notes on the same string keep the lower fingers on – in case you go back to those notes.

- To get a clear sound, press with the tips (rather than the pads) of your fingers. Press as close as possible to the fretwire.

Start playing

The easiest and most useful scales for *Beginner Plus* improvisation are illustrated on the following pages. These scales are also the exact ones required for the Registry Of Guitar Tutors Grade One electric guitar examination. If you find these scales very difficult to play you should review the previous book in this series (*Improvising Lead Guitar – Total Beginner*) before proceeding.

time to improvise

After each scale you'll find a set of chord sequences which are in the same key. These chord sequences are all featured on the accompanying CD.

Use the scale illustrated to improvise your own solo over the backing tracks; but make sure that you've read the preceding chapter on 'how to improvise' before you start.

It is advisable to listen carefully to one sequence of the backing track before beginning to improvise. That way you'll be able to get a feel for the musical style and structure of the sequence.

Use each scale as a vehicle to communicate the musical ideas and emotions that are within you.

Most importantly of all – enjoy youself and have fun…

Tony Skinner

Tony Skinner

E Minor

CD track 2

E NATURAL MINOR SCALE – 2 OCTAVES

E	F#	G	A	B	C	D	E
1	2	♭3	4	5	♭6	♭7	8

Practise the E Natural Minor scale and then use it to improvise some lead guitar over the backing tracks shown below.

Disco funk – CD track 3

$\frac{4}{4}$ Em | Em | D | D | Em | Em |

D | D | C | Cmaj7 | D | D ‖

Ambient groove – CD track 4

$\frac{4}{4}$ Em | C | Em | C | Em | D | C | Am ‖

E Blues

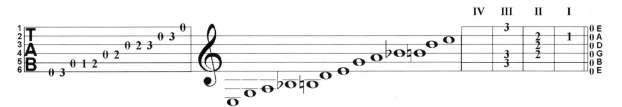

Practise the E Blues scale and then use it to improvise some lead guitar over the backing tracks shown below.

Rock 'n' roll – CD track 6

$\frac{4}{4}$ E7 | E7 | E7 | E7 | A7 | A7 |

E7 | E7 | B7 | A7 | E7 | E7 ‖

Country rock – CD track 7

$\frac{4}{4}$ E7 | E7 | G | A7 | E7 | E7 |

G | A7 | G | B7 ‖

G Major

CD track 8

G PENTATONIC MAJOR SCALE – 2 OCTAVES

Practise the G pentatonic major scale and then use it to improvise some lead guitar over the backing tracks shown below.

Country Ballad – CD track 9

$\frac{4}{4}$ G | G | G | Em | G | Em | Am | D ‖

Pop groove – CD track 10

$\frac{4}{4}$ G | Em | Am | C | Am | G | Em | Em ‖

 Major

Practise the A major scale and then use it to improvise some lead guitar over the backing tracks shown below.

Romantic ballad – CD track 12

$\frac{4}{4}$ Amaj7 | Dmaj7 | Dmaj7 | Amaj7 |

Amaj7 | D | E | E7 ‖

'60s pop – CD track 13

$\frac{4}{4}$ A | A | E | E7 | D | E | A | E7 ‖

 Minor

CD track 14

A PENTATONIC MINOR SCALE – 2 OCTAVES

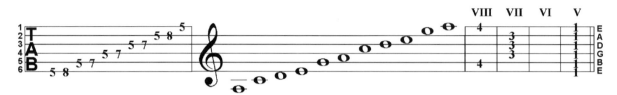

Practise the A pentatonic minor scale and then use it to improvise some lead guitar over the backing tracks shown below.

Melodic rock – CD track 15

$\frac{4}{4}$ Am | Dm | G | Em | Am | Em | Dm | G ||

Heavy metal – CD track 16

$\frac{4}{4}$ Am | G | G | Am | Dm | Dm | G | Em ||

Where next

Working through this book and playing along with the CD tracks should have helped you progress well onto the lead guitar playing road. If you want to move 'further on down the road' then you should get hold of a copy of the next book and CD in this series: 'Improvising Lead Guitar – Improver Level'. It will guide you carefully through the next stage in your improvising journey by introducing a wider area of the fingerboard and essential lead guitar techniques, such as slurs and string bends. If you enjoyed this book, you'll find the next one even better!

make the grade

By working through all the material in this book you will have covered all the requirements of the *Scales* and *Lead Guitar* sections of the Registry of Guitar Tutors Grade One electric guitar examination syllabus.

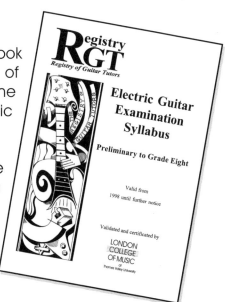

To pass the examination, and to make sure that you develop your guitar playing in a structured and comprehensive way, you should study the other sections of the examination syllabus. These are:

- Chords
- Rhythm Playing
- Musical Knowledge
- Aural Awareness

Studying all these topics will greatly help you improve as a guitar player. The books shown overleaf are specifically designed to help you develop your guitar playing in these areas. You can order them from your local book store or directly from the Registry of Guitar Tutors.

Further study

Electric Guitar Playing

(Grade One) by Tony Skinner

Can you make the grade? Find out by reading this book!

If you learn to play all the things contained within this book you will be able to gain an internationally recognised qualification in electric guitar playing. It covers all the areas of guitar playing and musical knowledge that you need to pass your Grade One examination.

Even if you're not interested in exams, the Handbook will help you to become a much improved guitarist and fully rounded musician.

Rhythm Guitar Playing

(Book One) by Chaz Hart

Is your rhythm playing as good as your lead? If not, this is the book for you!

It contains over 30 chord sequences for you to practise, and gives plenty of advice and tips on how to improve your rhythm playing.

All the chords required for the Grade One examination, and many more, are fully covered in this book.

You can order these books from your local book store or directly from the address below.

Registry RGT
Registry of Guitar Tutors
Registry House, Churchill Mews, Dennett Rd, Croydon, CR0 3JH, United Kingdom.
Tel: 020 8665 7666. Fax: 020 8665 7667
Website: www.RegistryOfGuitarTutors.com   E mail: mail@RegistryOfGuitarTutors.com